QUICK & EASY

SCROLL SAW

TOY PATTERNS

Over a dozen original full-size patterns

ROCKIN' ROLLERS

JOHN W. LEWMAN
CYNTHIA A. LEWMAN

Wood toy plans and patterns created by Toymaker Press are the best royalty-free toy plans available anywhere.

That's right. Toys built from our toy plans and patterns are royalty-free. You can build as many toys as you like for either personal or commercial purposes.

The plans and patterns in this book can be photo-copied for personal use when making work patterns for building the toys.

The plans and patterns are copyrighted and cannot be distributed or shared for free or for any commercial purposes.

Toymaker Press, Inc.
Shawnee, KS 66216
www.toymakerpress.com

ISBN 978-1-4507-0047-4

9 781450 700474

QUICK & EASY
SCROLL SAW
TOY PATTERNS

ROCKIN' ROLLERS

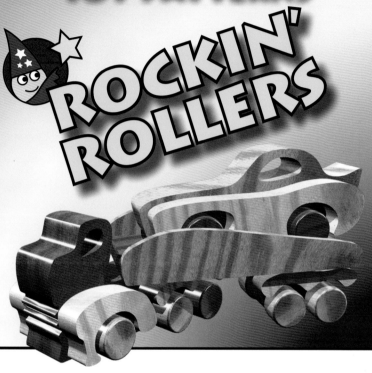

FREAKY FORD COASTER

This Freaky Ford hot rod from the Forties is fun to make and even more fun to play with. It is easily constructed from standard pine lumber and hardwood dowels. You can make several of these little jewels on a weekend. Lightly sand the surfaces and edges after assembly with 100 grit paper. Give it a couple of coats of polyurethane clear to keep it fresh and bright.

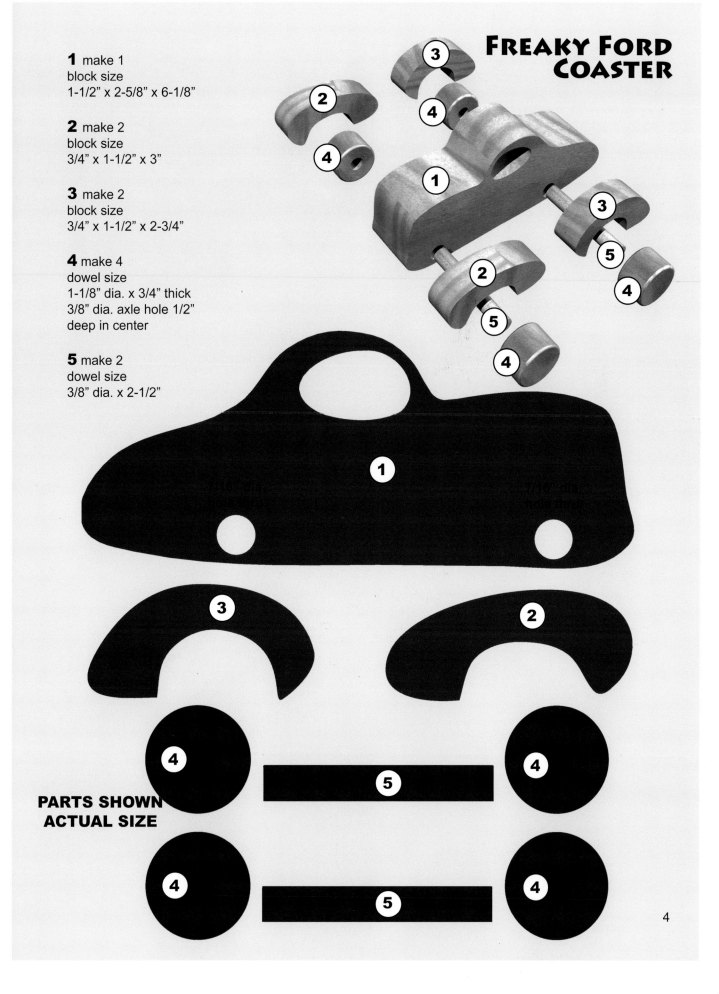

FREAKY FORD COASTER

1 make 1
block size
1-1/2" x 2-5/8" x 6-1/8"

2 make 2
block size
3/4" x 1-1/2" x 3"

3 make 2
block size
3/4" x 1-1/2" x 2-3/4"

4 make 4
dowel size
1-1/8" dia. x 3/4" thick
3/8" dia. axle hole 1/2"
deep in center

5 make 2
dowel size
3/8" dia. x 2-1/2"

PARTS SHOWN ACTUAL SIZE

7/16" dia. hole thru

7/16" dia. hole thru

4

FREAKY FORD TAKE-APART

Toddlers love to take apart and re-stack this little racer for hours. Make the body of common pine 2 x 4's. The axles and wheels are hardwood dowels cut to length. Leave it unfinished or color it with non-toxic paints and stains. A couple of coats of polyurethane clear adds a nice sheen and keeps the toy clean and bright.

FREAKY FORD TAKE-APART

1-2-3-4-5 make 1
block size
1-1/2" x 2-5/8" x 6-1/8"

6 make 4
dowel size
1-1/8" dia. x 3/4" thick
3/8" dia. hole 1/2" deep

7 make 2
dowel size
3/8" dia. x 2-1/2"

**PARTS SHOWN
ACTUAL SIZE**

7/16" dia.
hole thru

7/16" dia.
hole thru

FREAKY FORD PUZZLE

The puzzle is constructed with 2 layers of 1/4" birch plywood. The backer board is a simple rectangle with rounded edges. The puzzle panel is the same size with sawn features. The outer frame of the puzzle panel is glued to the backer board. The individual pieces can be natural, stained or painted bright non-toxic colors.

puzzle panels
puzzle blank 1/4" x 6-5/8" x 8"
puzzle backer 1/4" x 6-5/8" x 8"

PUZZLE SHOWN
ACTUAL SIZE

puzzle panels
puzzle blank 1/4" x 6-5/8" x 8"
puzzle backer 1/4" x 6-5/8" x 8"

CHARGER COASTER

The Charger captures the excitement of the muscle cars produced in the late sixties and early seventies. It is easy to saw and quick to assemble. Kids love the wow curves of the Charger and like to have several on hand to race and to share with their friends.

1
make 1
block size
1-1/2" x 2-1/2" x 6-1/4"

2
make 2
block size
3/4" x 1-5/8" x 5-1/4"

3
make 4
dowel size
1-1/8" dia. x 3/4" thick
3/8" dia. hole 1/2" deep

4
make 2
dowel size
3/8" dia. x 2-1/2"

CHARGER COASTER

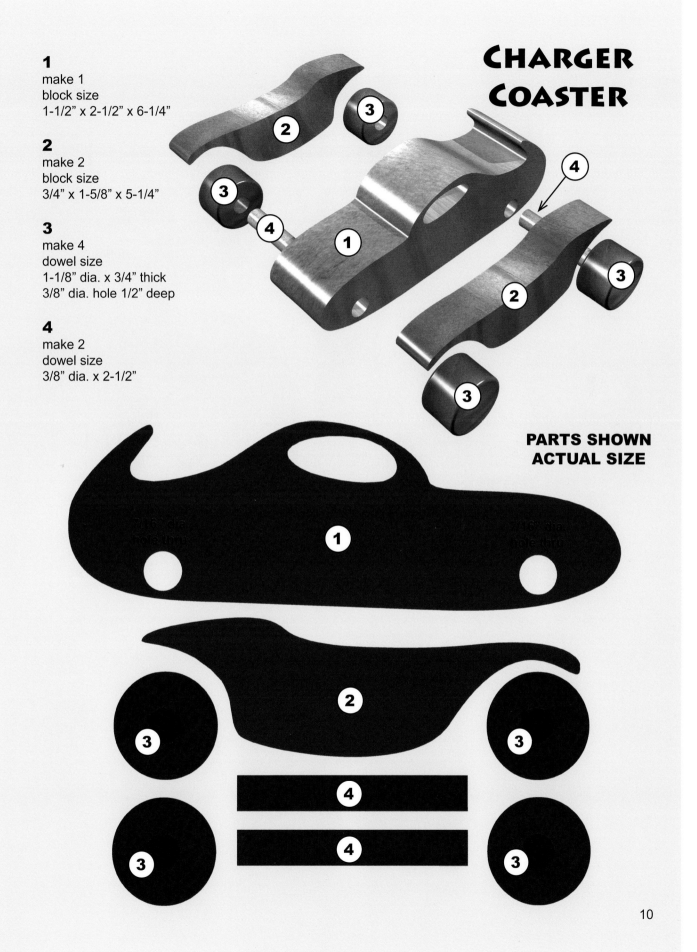

**PARTS SHOWN
ACTUAL SIZE**

7/16" dia.
hole thru

7/16" dia.
hole thru

CHARGER TAKE-APART

Kids love to play with building toys and this little Charger helps them learn new skills and tricks. The body is made of common pine 2 x 4's. The axles and wheels are hardwood dowels cut to length. Leave it unfinished or color it with non-toxic paints and stains. A couple of coats of polyurethane clear adds a nice sheen and keeps the toy clean and bright.

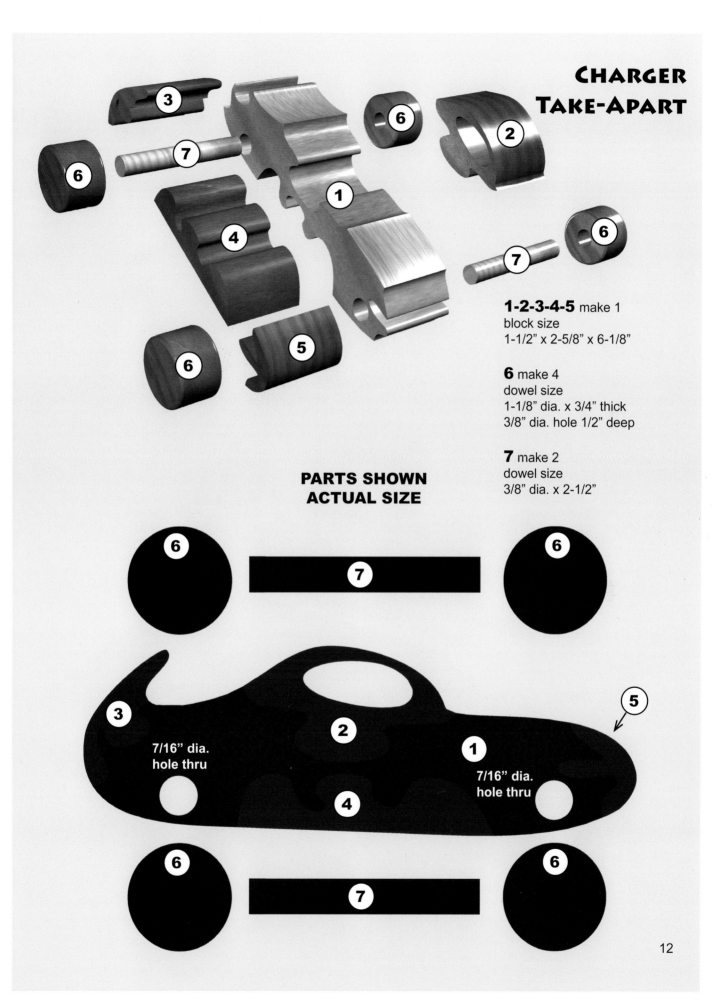

CHARGER TAKE-APART

1-2-3-4-5 make 1
block size
1-1/2" x 2-5/8" x 6-1/8"

6 make 4
dowel size
1-1/8" dia. x 3/4" thick
3/8" dia. hole 1/2" deep

7 make 2
dowel size
3/8" dia. x 2-1/2"

**PARTS SHOWN
ACTUAL SIZE**

7/16" dia.
hole thru

7/16" dia.
hole thru

CHARGER PUZZLE

The puzzle is constructed with 2 layers of 1/4" birch plywood. The backer board is a simple rectangle with rounded edges. The puzzle panel is the same size with sawn features. The outer frame of the puzzle panel is glued to the backer board. The individual pieces can be natural, stained or painted with bright non-toxic colors.

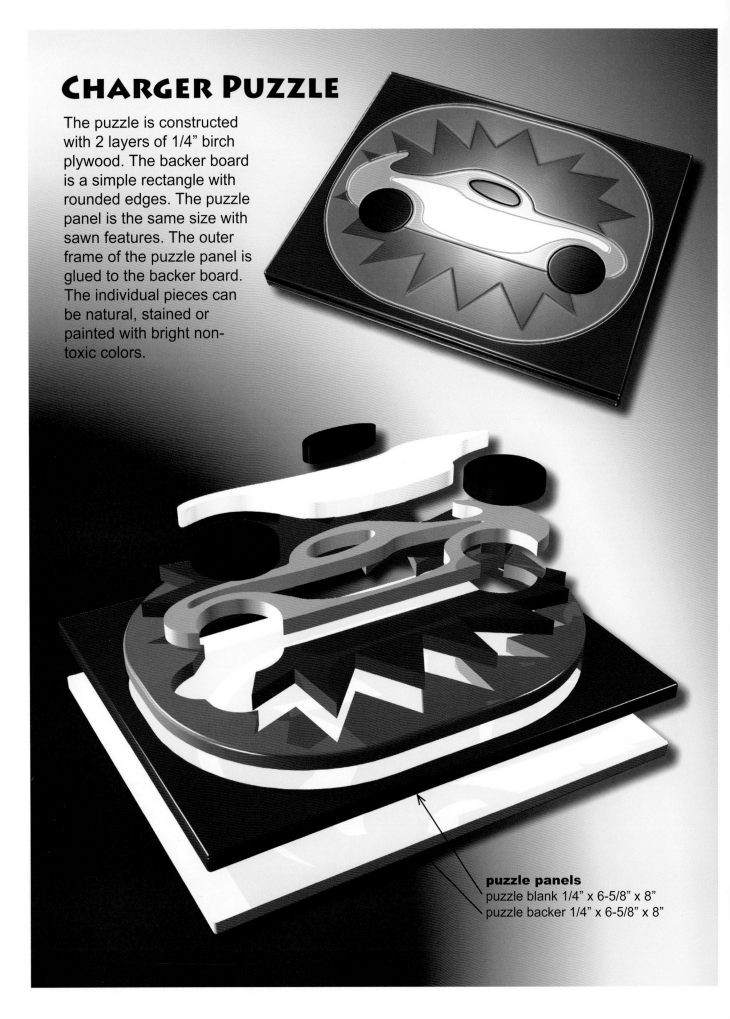

puzzle panels
puzzle blank 1/4" x 6-5/8" x 8"
puzzle backer 1/4" x 6-5/8" x 8"

CHARGER PUZZLE

**PUZZLE SHOWN
ACTUAL SIZE**

puzzle panels
puzzle blank 1/4" x 6-5/8" x 8"
puzzle backer 1/4" x 6-5/8" x 8"

14

STUDE DUDE COASTER

The Stude has become the custom car of choice for many nostalgia buffs. This version is fun to saw and is a snap to assemble. The fat fenders and sleek, low top make this a popular toy for custom car enthusiasts.

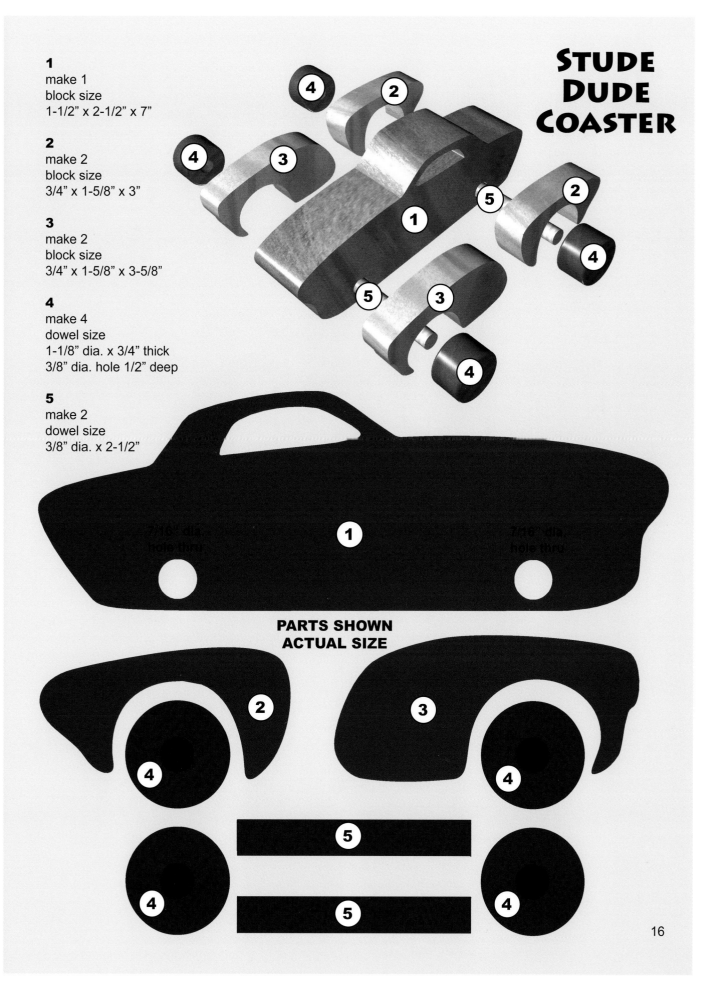

1
make 1
block size
1-1/2" x 2-1/2" x 7"

2
make 2
block size
3/4" x 1-5/8" x 3"

3
make 2
block size
3/4" x 1-5/8" x 3-5/8"

4
make 4
dowel size
1-1/8" dia. x 3/4" thick
3/8" dia. hole 1/2" deep

5
make 2
dowel size
3/8" dia. x 2-1/2"

STUDE
DUDE
COASTER

7/16" dia.
hole thru

7/16" dia.
hole thru

**PARTS SHOWN
ACTUAL SIZE**

16

STUDE DUDE TAKE-APART

Kids enjoy assembling and taking apart this dynamically designed stacking toy. The body is made of common pine 2 x 4's. The axles and wheels are hardwood dowels cut to length. Leave it unfinished or color it with non-toxic paints and stains. A couple of coats of polyurethane clear adds a nice sheen and keeps the toy clean and bright.

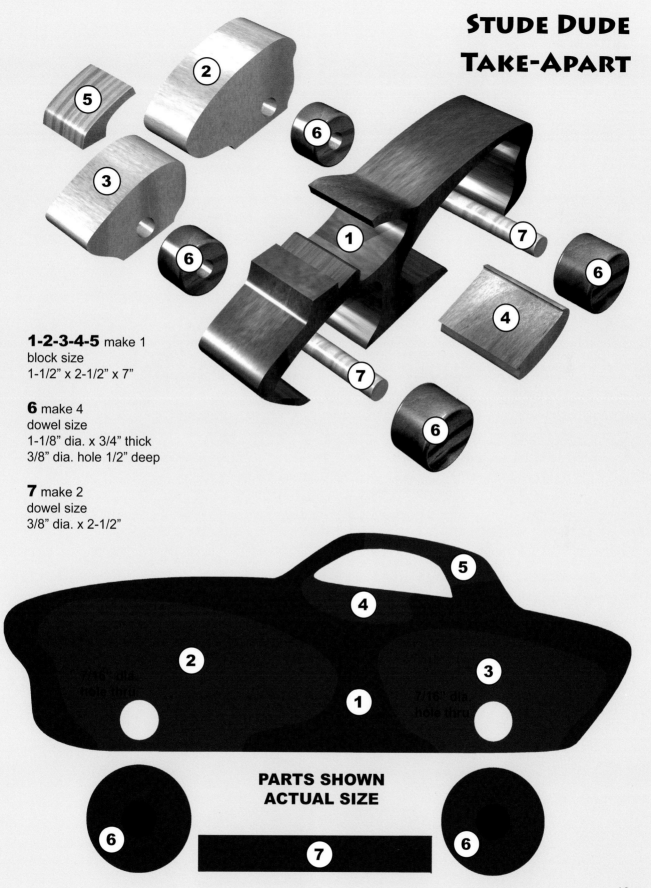

STUDE DUDE TAKE-APART

1-2-3-4-5 make 1
block size
1-1/2" x 2-1/2" x 7"

6 make 4
dowel size
1-1/8" dia. x 3/4" thick
3/8" dia. hole 1/2" deep

7 make 2
dowel size
3/8" dia. x 2-1/2"

7/16" dia.
hole thru

7/16" dia.
hole thru

**PARTS SHOWN
ACTUAL SIZE**

STUDE DUDE PUZZLE

The puzzle is constructed with 2 layers of 1/4" birch plywood. The backer board is a simple rectangle with rounded edges. The puzzle panel is the same size with sawn features. The outer frame of the puzzle panel is glued to the backer board. The individual pieces can be natural, stained or painted bright non-toxic colors.

puzzle panels
puzzle blank 1/4" x 6-5/8" x 8"
puzzle backer 1/4" x 6-5/8" x 8"

**PUZZLE SHOWN
ACTUAL SIZE**

puzzle panels
puzzle blank 1/4" x 6-5/8" x 8"
puzzle backer 1/4" x 6-5/8" x 8"

POWER PONY COASTER

The Pony cars created in the early sixties are going strong and are more popular than ever. You'll be pleasantly surprised how easy this version is to saw and assemble and you can make a whole stable of these little wonders over a weekend.

POWER PONY COASTER

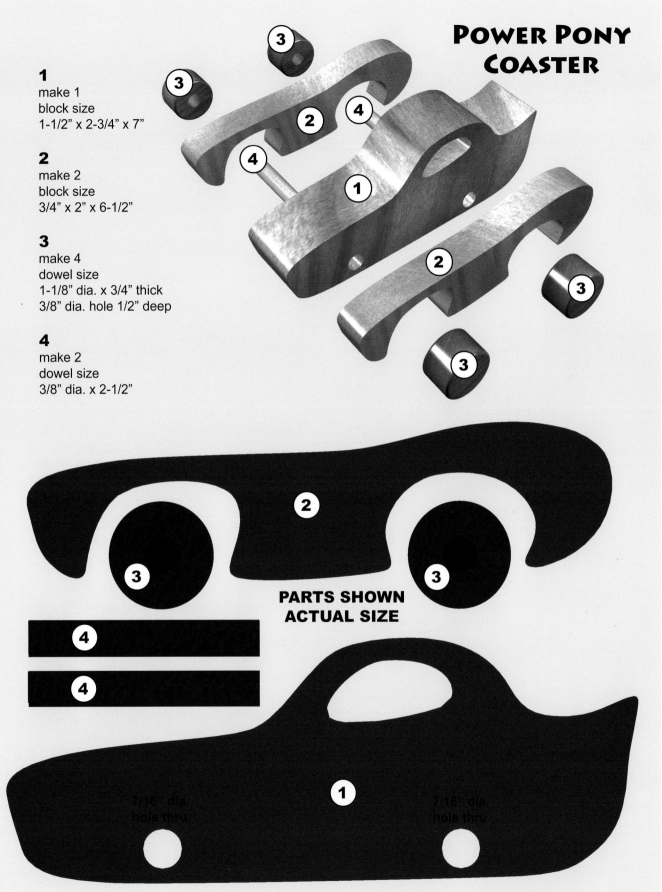

1
make 1
block size
1-1/2" x 2-3/4" x 7"

2
make 2
block size
3/4" x 2" x 6-1/2"

3
make 4
dowel size
1-1/8" dia. x 3/4" thick
3/8" dia. hole 1/2" deep

4
make 2
dowel size
3/8" dia. x 2-1/2"

**PARTS SHOWN
ACTUAL SIZE**

7/16" dia.
hole thru

7/16" dia.
hole thru

POWER PONY TAKE-APART

Kids enjoy assembling
and taking apart this
dynamically designed
stacking toy. The body
is made of common pine
2 x 4's. The axles and
wheels are hardwood
dowels cut to length.
Leave it unfinished or
color it with non-toxic
paints and stains.
A couple of coats of
polyurethane clear adds
a nice sheen and keeps
the toy clean and bright.

POWER PONY
TAKE-APART

1-2-3-4-5 make 1
block size
1-1/2" x 2-1/2" x 7"

6 make 4
dowel size
1-1/8" dia. x 3/4" thick
3/8" dia. hole 1/2" deep

7 make 2
dowel size
3/8" dia. x 2-1/2"

**PARTS SHOWN
ACTUAL SIZE**

7/16" dia.
hole thru

7/16" dia.
hole thru

POWER PONY PUZZLE

The puzzle is constructed with 2 layers of 1/4" birch plywood. The backer board is a simple rectangle with rounded edges. The puzzle panel is the same size with sawn features. The outer frame of the puzzle panel is glued to the backer board. The individual pieces can be natural, stained or painted bright non-toxic colors.

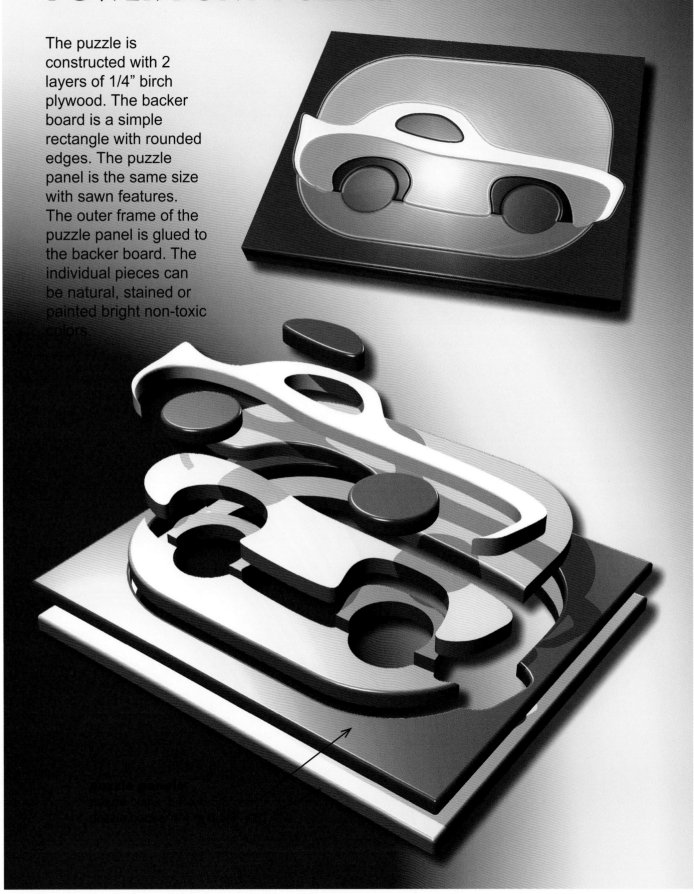

POWER PONY PUZZLE

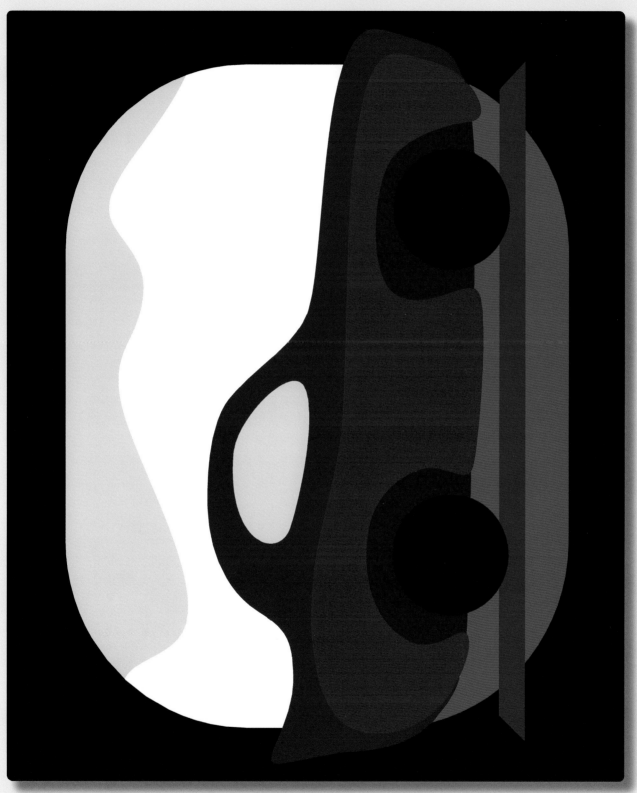

**PUZZLE SHOWN
ACTUAL SIZE**

puzzle panels
puzzle blank 1/4" x 6-5/8" x 8"
puzzle backer 1/4" x 6-5/8" x 8"

HiBoy Transit Coaster Tractor

The old HiBoys make a great transit for that precious custom car toy of yours. These classic trucks from the thirties and forties are a favorite with car crafters due to their flamboyant fenders and extreme proportions. This little model is so easy to make that you'll want to make your own entire fleet.

**HiBoy Transit
Coaster Trailer
Plan Set
see Page 29-30**

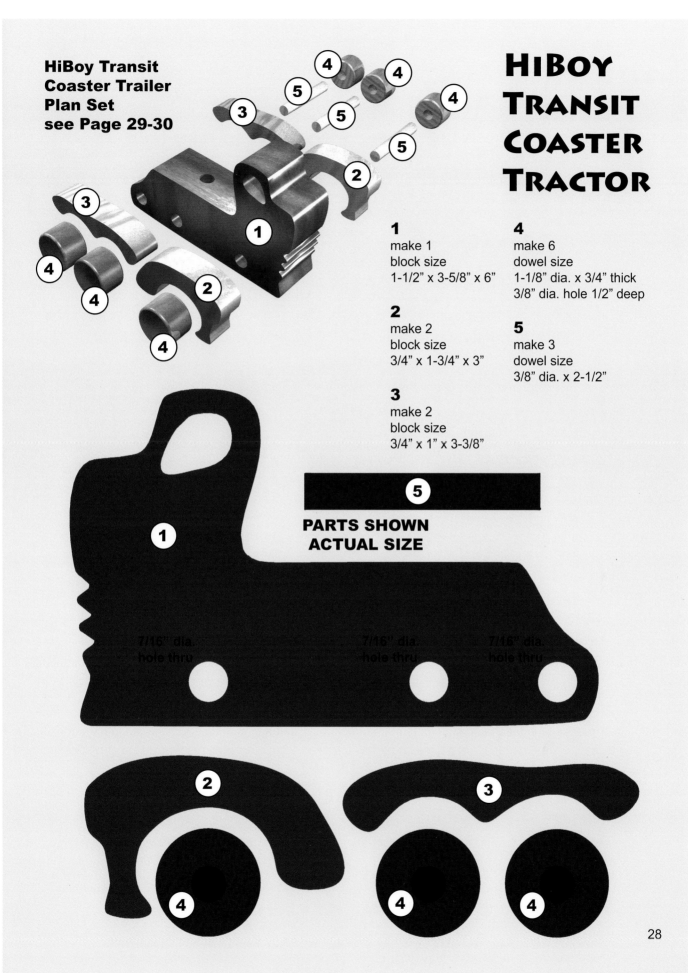

**HiBoy Transit
Coaster Trailer
Plan Set
see Page 29-30**

HIBOY
TRANSIT
COASTER
TRACTOR

1
make 1
block size
1-1/2" x 3-5/8" x 6"

2
make 2
block size
3/4" x 1-3/4" x 3"

3
make 2
block size
3/4" x 1" x 3-3/8"

4
make 6
dowel size
1-1/8" dia. x 3/4" thick
3/8" dia. hole 1/2" deep

5
make 3
dowel size
3/8" dia. x 2-1/2"

**PARTS SHOWN
ACTUAL SIZE**

7/16" dia.
hole thru

7/16" dia.
hole thru

7/16" dia.
hole thru

HiBoy Transit Coaster Trailer

The HiBoy Trailer is a highly styled loader with plenty of room for hauling your custom toy creations. Try your hand at modifying some of the curves to fit your taste and at creating a variety of custom cargo to be hauled.

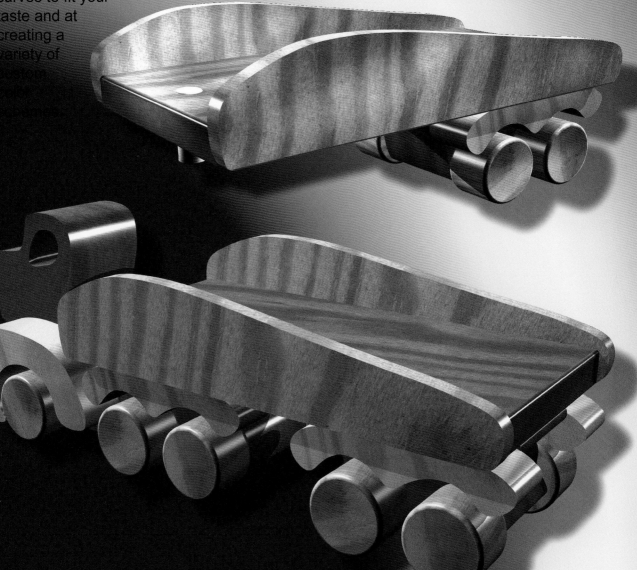

HIBOY
TRANSIT
COASTER
TRAILER

**HiBoy Transit
Coaster Tractor
Plan Set
see Page 27-28**

4

6

3

7/16" dia.
hole thru

7/16" dia.
hole thru

2

1

**PARTS SHOWN
ACTUAL SIZE**

5

7

5

1
make 2
block size
1/4" x 1-3/4" x 7"

2
make 1
block size
1/2" x 3-1/2" x 7-1/8"

3
make 1
block size
1-1/2" x 1-3/4" x 3-1/8"

4
make 1
dowel size
3/8" dia. x 1"

5
make 4
dowel size
1-1/8" dia. x 3/4" thick
3/8" dia. hole 1/2" deep

6
make 2
dowel size
3/8" dia. x 2-1/2"

7
make 2
3/4" x 1" x 3-3/8"

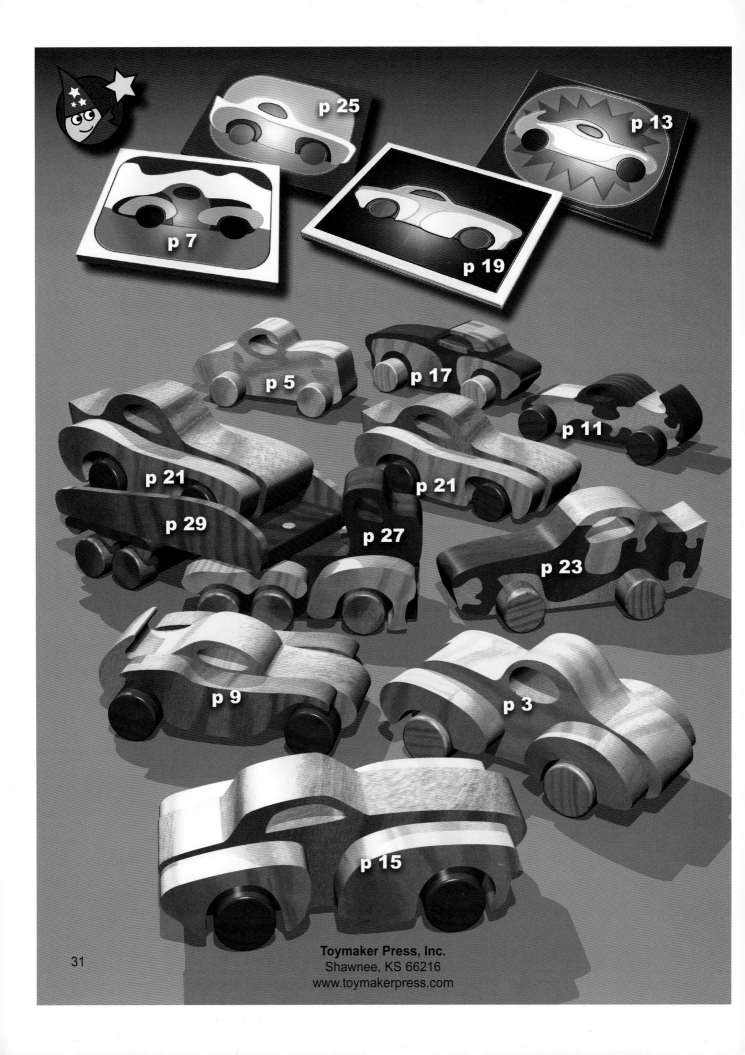

p 25

p 13

p 7

p 19

p 5

p 17

p 11

p 21

p 21

p 29

p 27

p 23

p 9

p 3

p 15

Toymaker Press, Inc.
Shawnee, KS 66216
www.toymakerpress.com